Rubies in the Forest

by
Phoebe Fillis

PublishAmerica
Baltimore

First printing

ISBN: 1-4241-2865-X
PUBLISHED BY PUBLISHAMERICA, LLLP
www.publishamerica.com
Baltimore

Printed in the United States of America

I dedicate my work to my children: Michael, Matthew, Melissa
and to my grandson, Zachary, and
to all those who may follow

I would like to thank my parents, grandparents, friends, husbands (both living and dead)—and my sisters—and all those who have encouraged, inspired and been supportive of my efforts over the years of my life...but also, most importantly, to give thanks to the beauty of the universe, the quality of the air and to all the spiritual and creative energies that have enabled me to be a receiver and a transmitter of all that which inspired me to record my time on earth—

1/12/06
Wakulla Gardens
Crawfordville, Florida

Contents

Know

Seek you ever
the love
that never cracks or breaks
but seeps
far into the dusty crevices
and wends its way
as you again discover
the beauty of a
rose.

Sunday

The essential Sunday streets:
Cars moving so slow.
People set to sea
with cowpeace
in their eyes.

Heaven Home

Moon hung high
My heaven's home
As it is below
so am I
above it now
Head held high
in the deepening night.

Benefactors

Star sigh sings in the
misted air
as we benefactors
to life
impair our love
by not loving.

We interrupt
the connected breath
to cry gasping
on the sand.

You, My Heart

You are my heart
singing a song
You click off
the melody
and memory floods
my steeple.
Trusting you
I become
the new direction—

Ecstatic

Ecstatic persona
not inebriate
the mind in violet
and chartreuse
overcomes
is its own high

Aftermath

(For Jim)

Down by the sea's sigh
near cobbled path
abides my cry and childlike laugh
Dwell shattered shells
I still can hear
where once we used to
dance and play
Dwell there the footprints
washed away.

Message From Beyond

Memory advises:
We are the sum total of all the parts;
But, if what we mean is meaning alone
then jasmine from the sweetest flower
would escape us:
the feel of twilight rushing through
the fingertips—
the stream of consciousness from birds on wing
would pass us by.

for we, are the chosen ones
with gift to see
beyond
the imagination

We are most realized in our
sleep perfecting
We are love transmuted to the poet's pen
Musicians of the soul's strains

We are the well from which the thirsty drink
overflowing with compassion—
We forgive, have learned to wait
to sidestep vile emotions
and soar with updrafts

We are triangles, diamonds, squares

The soft hands of guardian angels
lay themselves upon our shoulders
and teach us
the true gentleness....

WE ARE COME AGAIN
FOR RECOGNITION....

Roses of Expectancy

I live third world
in the new world today:
pie-eyed on beauty

I accept the signs and heed
every voice I hear—
Third world in the new world
today

I stop the flow,
putting finger to ear
so to stop dreaming for a love
I may not find—
but always I am looking out for
what is special
wild on honey hues
purple berry of my heart's
disconsolate self
that roars upwards
files miscellaneous
stored up and
pie-eyed.

I defy the spectacles of dust
upon my walls
Have no time for such
energy on my quest as I seek
pencil in hand,

a distant land stretched
from within
seeming fantastic
yet dim on detail…
splashed upon the brow
disconsolate

waiting and weeping in our
waking unto one another

The small impressions time makes
marking the sand
with barefoot soul….

Your Love

On a bonnie blue day
You
authored my love,
The seeds dispersed
through the swelling
of Spring

The day grew large
in my face
and all the small blossoms budding
returned their smiles
in this rarefied sunshine

Such perfection had not been
tasted
for a long time
Yet the day wore on
in profusion of flowers
and birdsong joy

The laughter of children's hearts

the slight swelling
rose to a crescendo
only to fall in
with a sharp word
an austere look
which punctured—

On earth the closest perfection
lies in the eyes of
a beloved
all else trembles

hurt children
have little faith
in the bonnie blue heaven
that spawned us all

They ignore those blue blues
that surmise us daily—
turning azure skies
grey, even in face of
unrefutable fact:

the blue burst abundance
of a shining love—
even the simple smile of
flowers that live
to die
without our love
or kissed sun,
yet come again

another day
are all the proof to know
the love is here for us....

When Love Allows

Oh you
who ever judge
the breath of each day

walk you ever through this
dazzling light
Allow sea air blow you
leaf like
through your moments

Be bird
Be sailboat
wind machine—
Joints loosened

Glide openly through the blue
and sunny apparitions
that guide you when

your love allows....

Blessing for My Friends

And should the recommended changes come about,
And should the heart beat louder than
the rock and roll drum:

Exercise that heart
Learn its position
Detect its changes

Do not let it falter,
Prescribe the changes to others
And go stick your head
under the water
and laugh in the fields of fiery hope

And hope that the bellows shall swell up
and fill again with new honey, new air
every day of your life!

Shards:

Who

will sit beside my chair,
cool in the afternoon,
Spoon away the hours to moonlight?

Whose sonata
will fill the blood of my life?

Thought Images:

Angel trumpetings,
the crumpled horn
of a unicorn tremble—
will ripen hours
as flowers

Pray
for all of us
Now

Leaves

tumble down from
shedding trees
to photograph
earth view
we cameras
do not
see.

20/20 See

The blind see more
through knowing hearts
than we, in our 20/20
blackouts…

Love Given

For all your love
you save and want
yet cannot capture
the golden ball of sun
in crystal glass
Cannot keep
less you give it away
to multiply upon the
light of daily sentences:
live refractions
cut glass prisms

over and over
and over again....

Sentience

To go up the mountain
and spread wings—
be bird:
I am what flies

I knife into watersplash
refinding surface to things
from liquid beneath
mingled with silvery fish, coral, sand:
I swim deep

To reach high to sun
feel points of petals
blooming cerise in noon heat:
I am what bursts flowers violet/saffron

I quake and shiver
to ancient beat
til body quiver
without thought to shadownote
I dance

To sliver notes in throat
like honey held to taste
on sun-drenched days:
I am what tastes rainbows
and I sing

I awaken from darkness
and find glowing embers
emitted from my mind's eye
coming into speech:
I meditate to find

I am sentient

To bathe between raindrops
and in the space between
blow out fragile wisps
that resonate-connect:

I am breath—

In this great universe
You may not realize
I am there
but
I am.

Your Soul

I'm just experiencing
my soul,
Teacher for this life
and along the caravan
of future shadows
as they fly
front of my face
Image to mirage
not unlike the
thump
of present circumstance.

Bearing Witness

The sunlight dashed upon the water
The testimonial trees
The shadows we cast—as spirit to body
The breath moving like a mobile—the winter leaves,
The touch of unseen hands,
in all that I see—
like sunlight on water
reminding me....

Observer

In the 2am cool
dark filled
bird pronounced Key West
painting
where a few late-nighters
stagger home
stuffing mouths hungrily
heading towards empty rooms—

I sit, unruffled
observed by none,
preserved in the clarity
of, after the party's been
spent....

Truth of Sea

Water-smoothed breath
lapping at the shore
of this very new day

We sit upon yet another
brother to that which has gone before
and plugging the old holes with
rounded toes
listen lively to the squeal of brakes;

The fish in schools
learn the way
telepathically
of that great spirit sea

Like me, mystery sea, you change
new clothes from moment to moment—

A great mother love of opal illusion

Always becoming

You are anything to the magic mood and
shifting wind of a time's whim…

A creator, always creating—

Therein lies your great consistency!

Oceanic

The stars
do not know me
or you
Yet, swallowed up by the current
I allow myself
full of life
to drift
dead man's float
part of all
now defined—
lost in space…

Birth

Here, far out
in the amniotic sea
the wet garden of weeds
urges your way back to shore
where tossed out
your body avoids
the sharp rocks
advances daringly through
a sudden rough current
gnarled from hustling winds

Congealed and
born again
you return
broken off
feet to sand
as to the rough spot
on the bottom of newly blown glass
you like to touch

Spot where the moulten umbilical
was severed
by the glass blower
who gave the breath
formed to break
for freedom sake

And so your birthmark
follows you
as the earth itself
is a tangible
and provides that
slight umber pull
to which you must
return

Now feel with your smooth
fish feet, little one,
that which is here for you
long after the sea
mentioned your coming.

At the Quarry

Swimming through a clear
deep pool of
salt water
we meet
eyes linked
for a moment
til you know
I am scraped clean
and new in
natural peace—

This is my secret
I share with you:
Hair slickered
over my face
dog like
peering up
as you hesitate
on the rock ledge—

The rays of a deep star
search
light through the depths
to sandmarl bottom
where you rest
meeting my heart
with your eye. . . .

Water Bearers

I take turns
pulling the long twisted rope
from the deep dark well
where the water yet is sweet
and will quench your dryness

A taste
and you are thirsty no more

Pull up the bucket
to discover
the simple thoughts of love let loose
and you

Drink with me now
for this life is
too short to desert

Drink of the clear and simple
nature of things—
Leave off the swirling images
that disturb

Love is enough
on a lovely day

The way is narrow but sure
and your cup
holds a cool
good drink…

Credo

Poet I am of land and skies and waters:
of rushing oceans that foam at the mouth
and of gentle streams that meander under country bridges
and of heavy skies leadened with everyone's hangovers—
with portents of rains and rages-stirring

I am poet of moment and poet of place
Poet of occasion and of inner scape
I comb expression to refine each
that it become part of your own
vernacular

I suck out the feeling of a place or a time—and its aura,
as some might linger long over a juicy morsel—
and I paint what happens there to define messages
hidden beneath the everyday motions;

I am poet of yesterday, living today,
Poet of people who have not the words
Poet of dumb animals and babies whose eyes beseech me
Poet of flowers: sweet smells and satin petals,
Poet of lovers, who long only for their moment.

I see the big and the small of it—poet that I am,
I see the bright songs of spring, shouted through meadows
and the somber guise of winter, suffocating in houses;
I am poet of open space and wanderings,
I am confined in my own space by myself
I am enunciated and claimed and totally loose and
unspoken—
I am wide and tall and also very very small

I am recognized by some, remembered by all;
I whisper and I scream, I write and I am quiet,
I know everything and nothing and I live life solo,
and with a multitude…a host, that guide me from inside
my tiny house with its big, big windows.

Poet I am, and I love and have loved…and I have not loved;
And I have hated and sidestepped and looked also in the eye of
my beholder and into the glare of enemy fire—

I am born again and again with each new day
I nurture and am always a mothering part of this earth—
One who must give it up—stand alone
a tree in the forest
that stands with others—but is its own.

And in the twilight breath of old friends and new
offerings,
I give it all up
so that in the measure of solitude
I gain again
the still small voice of my
own emotion….

9/02

Hindsight

Learn from what has gone before…
Words spoken clearly
at the end of the day

Pictures that come to you
like raindrops falling
on your forehead
where at the end of your time
you may learn
the great humility.…

With My Eyes

Open pigment:
stained glass window on the mind...
The sun carved
on your hand
and all that the world implies:

I ask you with my
eyes...

Are you a real friend?

Of the Flower

And people came
giving me their guts
since I didn't have any
Since I am but flowerfulness
that lifts with the wind—

Small breezes disturb my hair
as I move through
cool lips
upon my skin

I feel like an eagle
soaring into the vast and
beyond every living thing
in a strange tense
a formless swirling mass of
ebbing lights
a pulsating sun centering
mutable cycles

Bits of the whole
I am no one thing that I could
clearly see—
Call it cell division

vanity?

My catalyst:
friends

I am defining the line from
activity to indolence
above it all, I watch with humility
for I be in heart of the flower
flowing wild with the day wind
growing
in my transparency

I can see you there
with the wind in your hair
looking at me…

Hanging Loose

forget your commas
your periods
your capitals and
your margins

forget your blue lined paper
and your pinching sense

time to free wheel through
the white

let go
you will be watched
you are but child of the universe
skipping wildly on the wet streets
hair wired like antennae

there are no reserves with the great love
you are loved for your freedom
which is part of it all

so meet it with inner gaze

it shines out through your glitter
as you dance gladly down the town
smiling at any you meet
til the sun shines warmth on all of us
and you jump out of your "clothes"
limited only by the breadth

of your spirit
flashing
even as the bread rises
and the music makes a
soup of emotions
you can now enjoy

A Woodsy Clairvoyance

At day the focus to
shrouded trees
encased in spidery bridal veils
that the great ones
behind us, hide and go seeking
from amid the pink clouds
to see through the other side

Prehaps through veils of illusion
we think to hide the truth
from ourselves

And as in all things
of the nature
the message through beauty mirror is
to soften by the greater meaning
of how all are here to gather
in daily readers of the day
how to help each
in the caring and the doing
so we all do it
better

Continuity

Hi Ho, we travelers
moving momentarily
over the bridges
past the cities
into the wide open green

Through the morning's light
and into the afternoon rain
out the opened window of night
into our separate
consciousness
together

Will we ever know each other
some other time ?
Will we know ourselves
but randomly?

Life seeps in through
the closed windows
We leave behind what we
leave
and psychically some of it
is still registered
through every windy mile forward
into the marking of the future
unfolding as it
becomes

Sit Heart to Heart

I have a simple song
for all the children:

Sit heart to heart with me
and we can share a baked potato
and sing together
as we criss-cross fingers
and fashion newspaper things
with wool string
for May apple wings
to fly away on days
when it gets tough
and a walk in the wind
and a fling from a tree
seem a better thing…

Live Teddy Bear Love

Your angel children
are live teddy bears
who return your cuddling

They will fling one leg
over you in sleep—
Little feet
reminiscent of a
fish stage
with translucent toes
like opals, imbued with
morning light

Newborn kangaroolets
nestle in to address mother's pouch
and the tiny turtles
clabber down to the sea
for a first swim

and pink-skinned sightless kitties seek
mother's soft nipples

So we let our young suckle
and as they nurse from us
these live teddy bears
fill the hollow in your chest
you did not know you had....

Textures of Love

It is what lingers longest:
Images of your being a mother

Long after their first goodbye
and the fall from grace—
the residue of a baby's sweetness
shyly portrays itself
painted exquisitely on the canvas
inside your head

The profile in pastels

Baby addresses mother for
nourishment

Nothing fulfills that nurturing
a woman needs to give more
than this soft
dependancy

Like the exuding fragrance of a
cinnamon leaf
crushed in your hand
that you press, nose to palm
to savor
long after the freshness is spent

You recall the feel of that love
as it still exists
permeating
long after your little ones
are gone.

For Mica

Interrupted verse.
Cesarian entrance

Stranger in a strange land
Masai walk, carved cane in hand

A landscape pulsates

You are an interim character
Accept that you are vital

You are walking through cloudy mists
on grey afternoons
bringing an Aztec rainbow....

Poem on Michael's Hipness

Should you speak
tweakingly
on little pig's feet
pickled with prunes,
and dig the warbled beauty
of catatonic fears
then
come lie by the side of the wizard
who tells the stories of June
while looking through the floor
to the other side and
we can laugh
Buddhabugged
together…

To Supple Things

In belonging to all children
I learn the history of the eye
and of the spaces
filled with especially electric currents
that match the ins
with all the outs of things
in this world
and prehaps, in the other ones
too numerous to tell of here

However
being committed entirely to the smell of fall
rushing through the palm trees
and to the disturbing draughts of female air
that howl during hurricanes
and being also committed to growing entirely
human in my being
and to not being unlovely as a woman
by making comfortable the places
where we share our nesting quietlys
these short tempered days—

I know in my heart
whenever I sight a little duckling
or come upon a school of waterfowl
like the waddling geese upon the river's front—
I know how very deeply
every woman is obliged
breast and belly alike
to every small and helpless thing

And through the histories of the many eyes
that see
one must abandon the small flights
and the realization of nothingness—
for a coming of age
of all supple things—
the pure and simple animal naiveties that displayed
upon the faintest brow of the
smallest mouse—
must be allowed

How much one can learn from
mother cats—

Mother did you learn so well?
or was it instinct just
wrapped in many pretty tissue packages
for us all to see
upon the bare shelves
where we heard your fanciful chants?

A Pictured Moment

She is a woman
of the future
The future lies in her
She enacts it now
for future reference

Sword clanging straight ahead
purple cloak swooping
eyes ablaze
trundling through the undergrowth
so unsure of self
heart blazing righteously
tears blinding the way

A woman lost
A child lost
A moment passed
and in the future
A moment one inscribes

You are the god-awful spell
of springtime
thrashing winter away
with your brazen fury—
The future come to light
engendering children of
a stronger urge—

Shards:

for Matty

My missing Matty
I burn more sage
realize
never surrender
even when all my time
has been devoted to
yielding

for Connie

Connie's a
pistol-packin' momma
She'll tell them

even if her heart
is aching

Hot Rose in the Wild Woods

There was no place to lay her
so we put her in a fleeced dresser drawer
She came so fast
there was little time to prepare
I thought I was in for a test
but instead they put a gas mask
to my face

The first look was
"Oche Chongya"—dark eyes
piercing my soul

So tiny she was
her flesh hung like a coat
on a hanger
but once she brought in the milk
with those first hard sucks
the flow was smooth and
she plumped out in no time and
became the healthiest little creature

She would dance and play
for an audience
was dubbed: "Miss Lightbulb"
and twirled about like
a tiny dancer
atop a music box

A vivid rose blooming now
in her beloved forest
walking the lanes of life

finding her way from what I clumsily traced
Making her own path, step by step
Tiny dancer in the wilds of life

My daughter, my confidant
a Hanukkah light, kindling others
my daughter, my mentor
whose sweetness flows ever into me
my rose
she grows deeper and deeper
gracing this life with
her beauty....

Gone to Lace

Young bird, wind-spun hair
flyin to the future
full force behind the clumps of trees
mist rising from the waters
your duplicate

Hold on, hold on fast
to these joyous moments
that ventilate the soul

Days that form the background for this picture
now expressed in symbols

Mother weaves the blue silk
of perfection
calls it the link—
Median from heaven
to this earth:
A silk with rose-coloured
threads between the blue
through which a music echoes

You make this music daughter
now as you walk and enjoy
the musty woods
Spring is waiting to be born

her puff is sweet smelling
and there is saffron-coloured cloth
for you to wind around your
brown curls

as you sit between the pines
collecting leaves
gone to lace.

Window on the World

You are shyly
peeking in
unnoticed
but orchestrating
melodies none but yourself
can hear

You whisper at me
while I sleep and
scuffling through my day
I find you leave me quarters
with their face up
showing which direction
you are headed

You tame the hidden shrew
and rise to the purpose of your own
becoming
like a red satin cloak to
taunt a bull with
olé…olé

and you are
in mercurial hiding

the seclusion
becomes you
like briars and thorns that
keep the world out and you
in there, somewhere deep

You are not safe anywhere
my sweet
if you cannot come to dinner
and the sunset
with your fellows

You are not safe from
yourself
and the thoughts that can
disturb you
into night

only the flash of light—
that shaft that opens
a path
to the most high
can save you
if you would but reach out
Ask!

You

You're closer to heaven
then you think
Your wishes are heard
and granted

Like picking berries
you can reach out and
gain your dreams

Your songs are heard
Your prayers are answered
You are recognized
as a sentient being
here on earth…

Writing Poems

It breaks your heart
to write a poem
like the blood of an angel
carved into glass
on the white paper
of the undreamed

You move as in a trance
and try to record
the variety of music
as it plays over and over
in your special box
and asks to be released
spilling over like cream
into the glass of your defining
into the sweetness of divining

even in the terror of the day
even in the moment that cannot stay

Tao Mission

Comforter
Guide,
The white bird that soars with the
Phoenix
Grey chalk at the tips of feathers,
tracing a trail of smoke

A Tao for the lonely
wayfarer, seafarer, soothsayer
peacemaker

A way all men can
understand—
follow
A simple way
we indians
who can recognize
each other
know of
from the gut truth
of experience

A way to calm
seeing out the ocean's sky
from the wake of frothy waves
as they slap upon the shore
of your mind's cave
and echo into mine

where dreams of tomorrow
may disturb the divine spell
of our love
allowed....

Cancer Battle

(For Al)

He lies, half in and half out
restoring himself
arms clasped to his chest
his feet dry/emaciated
The noble warrior spent but handsome still
Much of the battle remains
much has been fought

He nibbles at the edges of life and
does not talk of death
though it comes closer
Only our good hearts and hopes
protect him from the ravenous ravages of
this dis-ease

The machines wear him down
to save him and
he apologizes to me

A life slips by
the life we have shared
So much a stranger from the man
who loved to fry me chicken
hair hanging that surfer way—
his casual manly grace

I saw him once as an indian prince
drenched in turquoise
and later, after my children were gone
he would always bring in a cup of tea
to greet the new day: "high tea"
and me with my early grouchies
and he with his "I love you..."

And now, the tears held in
or will not easily come
Our life together is altered
prehaps forever—
Our life is fighting and fatigue
and doctors and drugs
and the prayer that the good fight
will prevail and that
he won't get too grouchy—
that love will have its say
and he will be
a stranger no more...

To Unicorns

(For Gay)

Every which once in a while
is a purple rose
deep and burgundy
and most unusual
or an egg that comes out double
or an extra nut in the peanut shell
or some one who will love you
unicorn

And every once in a while
when you put your hand under the water
and pull up some unexpected oddment,
Think of me
perfect
like the one-of-a-kind cracks
on a Chinese vase—
rare and individual
entity of one—

So reach out unicorn
and do not doubt that we
like the clover of four
have our purpose.

For Monday's Love

As the clock turns
and quivers in my heart
marking out
the moment of the day
that I should see you yet
and small slivers of sunlight creep
into the recesses of my dwindling self
the plum-colored clothes of autumn
comfort me
during the long nights when
nakedness
would hold more truth
than all your words
or all of mine.

Tender autumn
sending sips of love
in between the grass
and negative bite of the time
Dandelions dare reach noddy heads sunward
and time's message grows less clear
with each succeeding "no"

How come the simple holding of hands
and kissing of lips
is not enough for us wasted lovers?
when there is that faith which splashes
itself reckless across the skies
at sunset
like a flowing, rose-haired woman
stretched out upon a canvas to dry.

You Are Roses

(For my teachers)

Roses, roses
Roses for your pillow, my love
Roses for your cheeks
and your eyes
and your clothes
and your sighs

Roses threaded on the air
and growing by the windowpanes
and hanging in great drooping
bunches
from wire baskets on the porch

Red, yellow, white roses
on the table with the very white
starched cloth and roses in your hair—
a perfumed halo of the great love

You are roses, my Lord
you are love everlasting
and at peace
with thorny arms
You are the garden and
the wall
and I am
but one rose…

Key West: The True Beauty Binds:

Daughter of Key West,
Blood ties pumped in
avocado treasure
looking into the lights
of baby eyes
even when the flood of
starched spectators manicures
the quaint funk
and silvered wood
to sanitary ethics

Daughter
you are tied to every hot pink
bougainvillaea
and tanned bicycle person
like the music that threads the air
You are tied to the island magic
wherever you go

Child of Key West
faded denim—your pride
the debaucheries here
elude you and
the faces that protrude
even with the soothing waters and
calling wind—
You were here to imprint
like fossil to rock
our own legacy, now part
of the island whisper
You bend your straw one time more
and pass the coral between your toes

Here where you flowered
where you learned the true sense of
friends
Here where home was
the most informal seclusion
Here your heart expands never to lose
its common touch

Key West holds you ever, daughter
for the island transmutes
its familiar theme
and you go on
to find new names
though the same cadence
directs you
The road follows you
wherever you go
even when you have no map

Some have to leave and return
to appreciate what you already know

Once you thought going away impossible
but now you find yourself
wide enough

Yet here is where your song distilled
like drops of coconut milk and
sea grape honey
And here you learned your
real name
grown into its own melody
giving rhythm and direction so that
now you are still that
refrain

you made while walking 'round the cemetery
and filling your eyes with all the
photographs you could see.

And you will return
ever and ever in your heart
and more
to peridot peace remembered
like to the bosom of a familiar lullaby
always different, yet
the same
on the tip of the tongue and
woven into the dream in your heart
Come from a place that has centered
a song for your life
Come from a place where peace and beauty
sunsets and palm frond vision
find you faithful
from a morning fresh promise
of sunbeams and palm shadows
caught for the moment
coagulated now to
a bursting joy
to be in the wind
or to feel the air at seaside
breathing through a spirited night
breathing through all the
dusty trails you take
wherever you find your
self
you will find that
focal point

to measure your life by.

Cemetery Town

for Cayo Hueso (Key West)

Around the cemetery
where the city grew
the wood is stronger than stone
and ghosts of ponds and meadows
and sugarcane, live on
in the old people's minds
scratching the veneer
where childhood glimmers
widen the eye

We are living legacies
passing on
shedding where we have been
but chameleon life sprouts from the old
seeking the new and never too long still

Scraped surface reveals
a layered history—stratified—
If we are our usual—too patient—here
we can make time stand still

Wood—like spirit
is steadfast and lives on
Bone-hard resins caught fast
glue and petrify
where rock, like flesh
will crumble…

Around the town
people live in houses

fashioned by ship's carpenters
wooden pegs as nails
and beneath the floors
lie the ancient dead
still leaving legacies and
first told tales of this island place

Some of these houses moved on
with their owners
though graves stood still

Passing over a river that was
a trail did wind from a church once
passed alley and canal
with soft dirt underfoot
before the automobile and asphalt,
Spanish laurels protecting
the floods of childhoods and
spirited ivy wending its way

A trail where tamarind resting places
were chosen by those who loved
to plant their dead
to favorite spots sheltered by
bougainvillaea umbrellas
jasmine whispers
and the freshest air blown
off the sea from many a mile to
be at your side—
This a trail once told
through a country peace
well lived
fresh still and mingled:
the contemporary with the antique…

Pressing close by picket fences
you walked and
all the walks are still told
in secret memory-filled nights
where just around a corner a forgetful
"city" stalks—
tree roots cracking stone pavements
into intricate mosaics
like time recorded to present
in grain swirls like eyes
that have seen yesterday and today
and may be remembered
tomorrow....

Living Lace

My thought
is but an echo on the
horizon
that stretches from purple
into blue and the endless
unaccountable white

It is a hairlike tickle on the cheek
of the great giant
who oversees
through clouds and into tree limbs
flailing in the wind
and puffing through the kites
on a stormy day

My small golden thoughts
edging leaflike
woven at the foot of a faery princess
pirouetting on a
rainbow sea

My thought is lost as soon
as it is invented to my mind
if I do not scribe it
and it invents itself as it goes
from out of the quiet lips of
one who sees and only hopes to know
such living lace....

Awakening

It was a wake-up call
your last day on earth
The sun rose
as you went down
Your spirit rose
eyes wide open
you were ready
to meet your maker
The sun rose and
you along with it
into the vivid path
the brightest patch of blue
that would be your new
home....

Translucent Wings

Even a frail odour
could persuade you
to remember
a poignant time

or the sharp lush poetry
like a piece of cheesecake
first bite on
bringing you to a
poetry place
where translucent wings
can fly

where the storehouse of treasure
abides within
our special compartments
needing but the trigger of an odour
any shred of a reminder
of where you are come
and to where you go
and when we all are

It comes full circle
making new pictures for
your tucked-away scrapbook
that ever-so-lavender guide
you subtle on your way
and without your knowing it
formulate the hidden day....

You Know Me

Richly laden
we speak of miracles
of the wings being spread
of the bird
wide winged and stretching
freedom jump
into the wisdom of
fools and

Of the mind opened wide
to the supernatural

You, who drool with longing
Know without knowing…
You know me

Her Dogness

(for Mi Ami Cockish/Kasha Michelle)

Her dogness
rises to the occasion
with black-eyed susans
bulging
Cream-of-wheat coat
to rise on hind legs
pirouetting
a dainty tip-toe circus dance
for crackers
to wedge in between
you and a couch arm
to press a furry cheek
against yours
when the yipping and yapping
are through
and her tongue is stuck
hanging out her mouth
unconscious—

Her dogness,
with rabbit ears and nose
twitching
suddenly lounges back
Marilyn Monroe
in midst of a tooth to tooth
belly to belly
when filled with the scent
of a dog friend close by
to follow, lead
and dance all about with
the grace of snow flurries or

like children loosened
from a winter's bedding
rolled out to play

Yet here when she lies in my arms
jowls sagged
rounded forehead cocked back
begins a new day of love
even the children deeply consider
baubles tossed aside…

Sunshine Song

I take the stuff of life
the light fluffy unseen clouds
that float in front of your face
I take it and form it into
something prolific
something that grows and
has tenacity...like onions
and mud

I make poems
and sometimes a song
will occur
something you could dance to

The shiny patches of silver
and gold from each day
The whistling trees
the pure blue sky
A patchwork, my poem
to make something beautiful
you could suppose

Then clocked inside
with books and papers
cut off from the spirit of life
that frees me always
in my body, heart and mind
I perceive my fellows
from a distance
looking out my window—

There, a straining upwards
as with flowers
Here, tears held back
to a knowing
or the lifting of an eye
towards something bright
something new
something varied
something you
could remember
like a song

Wishes of Silk

Wise, so wise
the heart that reflects
love—
See it in the eyes
in the smile
in the tilt of the head
the opened palms
receiving light

You and I are
moonlight lovers
We swim through the darkness
and find little stars of delight
and the glow of moonlight
wraps you up in gentle silk
to lay you bare
for all to see
your luminous heart

All things so touched
respond in kind:
If you love
you will be loved
and if you care
you will be cared about
and so

It is the rhyme of the
universe
that keeps us flowing

from one empty room
into another
searching for the feel of
pure silk....

Cities 'neath the Sea

From there to here
is not so far away
You could still hear
the cry of a soul
from the depths of the sea
same as today
still could imagine the
embrace of
lovers fleeing
or a washerwoman's song
or a carpenter's plight

You still could feel it
from here to there—
the cities 'neath the sea
where once we were
meant to be
and now in our
advanced stage
we come to know
that it is not really so far
away from there to here
despite centuries and
Atlantian dreams...

The Windy Pass

Come walk with me
into the green wind of life
and please hold my hand
Tell me what I need to know

I cavort with gypsies
and climb great pines
to see squirrels squatting
far below
on the green grass of this
Monopoly board where we
play at being

Should the wind whisper promises and
miracles
as we sway back and forth
bending rocking
yielding
to the sound of the waves
as they lull by this
well-defined coast
then, branch out your life to mine
do not judge me for the holes we are
all meant to have
in order to be wise

It is the friendships help mend
these painful times
and you will not be disappointed if
your opened end
seeks the windy pass
for more air, light and
more love.

On Writing

Writing is a
quiet way of talking

to wander halfway between
the shores of extraordinary
mind-locked love
or to exude the moon
to our ever-silent
companions

we each a separate particle
that defies evolution
determines, without fortune,
a circuitous path
to discern the caterpillar's enigma
share the indolence of sun
the restless spirit of wind
the chameleon face of sea

to ever concoct description of
the quest for the holy grail of
silently perfected and forever told
fictions…

Poet

At the point of emaciation
we meet
and you claim me for
my disparaging awareness
None like it you say
across this great land
of withering tulips

For behold
I am a finder
ever seeking new
eccentricities
I come upon the most unusual
rose notes—while segments paint themselves
upon my brain
in separate harmonies

I conduct the brass band
with a twig of balsam
The cries of children heard together
for a special oneness

Enter, my wall
A wall forms
enveloping the outside
in
to a great encasement
of the many pebbly churnings
that crowd out the plumb cheeks
of every newborn day

How skinny I become
so full of myself within
I shrink on the outside
pointing to the long finger of
extenuating circumstance

But eating still the rich fruits
of poetry pitted on the tongue
I realize my meaningful diet
pruned to bite
and landscape imaginative trees—
sparkling violets—
within the great void....

Inner Freedom

My mind
like a cave—
images painted
on the wall
Spreads a vista
primitive
wishful
filled with gold
from Van Gogh
and beyond

I am a multiple
personality
talking to
itself
I eat the fruit of
Cezanne

I invite you
welcome your eyes
to illuminations
as sky and cloud
become your
room of rounded
vision

This to explore
without the
usual
confines of
rented rooms and
one-cent signs....

Dancing Spirit

Here in the breeze
under the old coconut trees
It shall come to pass that a
delicate dancer
shall cross our path
Slip in through the front door
and enliven the party with a snap
and could be angels watching
shall give the word
telling of the specialness
knowing nothing
can bring—
of the holes
through which can pass
gossamer silks and dreams
so pure
only a child could
imagine

And as the last bells toll
their spell
of delight and solidarity
and the breeze continues
to cool the sweat
breathless
so too shall come
the great discovery
that we are ever free
in our hearts when
we are loving

all of it
or any of it
whenever it comes
to our door....

God in All

Loving everybody
in place of ONE
I tear off my animal coats,
my furs and teeth and
outer expression
to pare to the grassy heart within
common to all

It is this heart
I would most wish to give
should the light
shine through me of a moment
and give itself
to you.....

Knowing

We do not know
why the wild weeds grow
endure
far beyond the slivers of
rose and honey day dawn
Do not know how with night
absence of light
can symbol the end of one life
beginning of another

We do not know
how the faint spark of a man's heart
causes a drum to beat
at sight of one in particular

We do not know how
but that it happens
through kindred beings—
the guardians of each
form sacred bonds
the mind of man can't know…

Growth from Illusion

In a somewhere land
between time and the last peppermint days
A few grey hairs imparted their tale:

Far, far below the melting narrows
between the folds of dawn
and the evening's downy end
the small surprised shadow on the wall
wistfully handed over into my keeping
a mushroom, poisoned with hope
for a new day
before the elder had its cue
spurning the characters and
the plot
for confusion
wherein the purest melody reigns....

One Eye to See

Opening the door wider
more air arrives by the minute
for it shall be told
that the dead sing too

Floundering in with dead lady's bouquets
and stuffed rag dolls
the wider jar, the more
air to fill

Each story revealed through
ivory fingers
nails buffed that
reflections might shine

One eye to see in
One eye to see out
from the greenhouse
where feeding from blooms of
lavender and rose
we watch the clock in the sky
sending down
mute messages....

Survival Recipe

How does the ancient cocaroach
survive
beyond the measure
of those greater?

He can eat doodoo
and like it!!!

Prophecy

Silent chromosomes
recall the past each man forgets
only they know how long it will be
and how much we will give
for the ending
so silent
not even the ants can feel it
An ending so enormous that
it is all endings foretold of
this protracted universe—
and all the mimicries of
reflected sorrow
shall not detain its
"Once Upon a Time..."

Love Is Not Enough

Sometimes love is not enough
for too much sun
can rot the flower
and too much rain
drowns it
and all your tears
washed away
mean nothing
but unsung songs
without words
that get lost in the wind
of everyone else's laundry!

To the Next Level

Born for each other
we forget
what once we knew
remembering what we have
to stoke it up
so it flashes
reminds
that what was left behind
is not entirely lost
but insteps in the steps you
take to the new day ahead

While imagery is best left
to chance vision
melted into all the hills of happiness
we hope for
we select the peachy hue
without the weights
from yesterday's blunders
to buoy us on

holding to the reminders
of what was lovely
so that what arises
will come upon us
in the right frame
from the good essence
that does thrive
on our love
knowing of that still
hopeful song
never entirely lost…

Love's Energy

Like a bellows
I will fill your house
with prayer light
of the high vibration
Outline all the furniture with
blue iridescence

I wish you white light
and golden light
to surround the darkness
of any musty retreat
and prove to you
the existence of
magic

I will sing songs to echo
through and into the relativity
of time and space—
My windpipe quivering
all my vital organs
harmonizing

I will envision your heartiness
in the light's reality
and you will feel it
even if you cannot see it…

Butterfly Light

I thought I was a guide, a doghearted spirit
a being under pressure with
the universe
due to my inner exploration

I am testimonial to the lamps of love
The light according to Van Gogh

And as I empty of light
shedding exoskeleton
I bud forth in butterfly gladness
and the natural electricity
arrives....

Life on the Totem Pole

I prefer pictures to words
but the words keep coming
Phrases and images
mated
for a special sound
even I do not wish to
separate

I hope to gain tongueness
to lick the sweet of my existence
and the eyes to see the clarity
behind every glistening
shadow
where I peer
through the darkness
seeing my own
blind space…

Synopsis

This life is
not meant for the faint of heart
my friend

You crush poems into your pillow
2 o'clock

and the miles roll by
even when you're asleep
and trying to forget

This life is not easy
not easy my friend
but
worth the miles
and the poems that come
along the way....

To the Light

In the dreamery land
where we wander through
a yellow wood
I spy a rubber tree to climb
one that will bend with our ways
And the rains come down on us
to provoke our intellects
stimulate our mind's eye
to see the true vibration
coming into its own

Becoming one and a part of our
gesticulation
as we go to do our thing
we race toward the crumbling
should it come

Shine the amethyst and the silver
Shine the marrow of your love's delight
This a light that will not die
Its glow gives faith to man
in the midst of insanity
is a light that never wavers
not even in the strongest winds

Fluted through the reedy throats
of mutant followers

this light of our times
all the time
Shines even if we have
forgotten
we remember
the light of all life and being
the light of ages
the justice of it all....

When Time Stands Still

When time stands still it makes a music happen
Makes a gladness billow in the heart
Registers a truth for all moments
Makes of itself, a reckoning of hammocks
Time without the figure of your words limiting the
second finger of wishes that could not congeal

This moment sits and sweetens the morning air
with handmade, homemade perfumes you would remember
It scents the current of doubt with the new
fragrance of tomorrows yet to be
New to the old research of this and yesterday

Time taking its course upon the source of rivers
rocks, earth
and the radical changes of mountains, minds, and lakes
Time meaningful, time passing, and time standing at attention
into the sequence of a new day's quest for peace

A peace of willow trees bending
with the felt sigh of afternoon
falling light to the lips and into the grass…

A Schma Yisroel

We are an embattled peoples
we have fought long, hard
to be counted in
We have traversed this earth
seeking friendship
acceptance
and a simple olive branch

We would sing
we would dance
and we do among ourselves
but
there is a cloud of serious measure
hangs over our heads
Knowing so many of us
lost, uncounted—forgotten
to the swords of hatred
and indifference

those who bully
provoke—hate
exist
today and in every
time
and the lesson repeated

We know full well how
the dragon can raise its
beasty head
and rage fires
again and again
on the unsuspecting

Schma Yisroel—still we pray
We are an embattled people
hoping always to join
in the peace
and the love
We do not have to excuse ourselves
for wanting human understanding
for the task always set before us
as scapegoats and victims, when
warriors, entrepreneurs, intellectuals
and artists we have always been—

Our test from the creator
to exact our faith
may be our greatest gift—
to hold on high
without arrogance
but with pride—
and in peace
our beliefs and traditions

To endure
to keep the faith aglow
and aflutter
and to know that under the skin
we all be sister and brothers
come to light
soul to soul—
and

if Christ were come again
he would count himself
among us....

Whispers of Immortality

Valentines Day '82
(for my father, Wm. B. Redner)

Orlando, my twin sister, sits besides me
sketching a beautiful face
from a magazine
She is expert

I work imperfectly
from life
to know there is no
final death
when the body has moulted

Only the flutter-winged flight
of wind-ruffled breath
A swift-flowing current upon the smooth
surface at Lake Eola.
The fountain sprouts foam and misted dancers
convoluting in the spray
The birds hearken to the water's edge
and a voice swells in cantorial tones
Oming with the squeech of birds
as passersby and the curious
promenade, Sunday like
amid azalea array

Orlando again: once silent and heart cracked
young ones defined their lived time—
I am she who waits
for all things
I am she who waits
for friendship
and to be a friend

to swimming birds
and little ones strolling
under the sun's strong gaze
I am she who waits for love
and loves
as love may come
And I am still she who sits
observing life:
The black, the white, the warm
the cold
Masters of planet earth
homebound here in old down home
Orlando
Holier than thou—

We who have been crunched here
We who have also felt the Seurat serenity and
stately peace
of mankind manicured—
unruffled—uneasy—
We who observe the distrust
yet trust them still
as the shell cracks
In kindness, we call out:

Oh, spread your wings man
Switch the channel to L I F E
we do not live by bread alone

There are some master yogis, I hear,
you cannot take their picture
for they have to command their spirit
be present
they are spirit first
those masters

They know all things of this world
are left behind
once the bird is freed
to skim the lights upon
the waters beyond
and immerse the feathered being
to leave but shadow behind
melting in the all light

My dear father, you are with us more now
that you are gone
I hope you can contact
those whose name it is
a blessing to know
Prehaps in the ethers high above the
snowy Himalayas
the real sojourn awaits all
who seek

There someday in timelessness
a rendezvous

This a day of hearts broken
I reckon
and hearts breaking and
hearts disappointed and
hearts sharing…
beating at one
with the tremor from
the great seismologic love
of the one verse….

Reading Life

The lightning bugs
move through the night
like headlights

The headlights
search through the night
like lightning bugs

Look, says the teacher,

Listen, says the night

Read life
and know....

Sweet for the Day

Be your own chocolate
I say
Relish those rich moments
alone with the beauties
of overhanging trees
and freshening breeze

be sweet to yourself
and allow the deep taste
prevail

You need this
it is your life

It is your treat
for the thin times

Yesterday's Crazyquilt

(for the one who shared my childhood)

On this August day
riding away from
tribal factors
I assume again
the role of observer

You, my counterpart
overindulging
your nurturing
You calm yourself now
from furious winds
that once scattered our purpose
to band together
in separate unity

One of us counts the strokes
the other swims
I say, think the best first
before testing the worst
for we can hear the sea
in the spiral shell
and you cannot doubt it
intended to be
ear shaped
so listen now
with inner heart open:

Standing in front of the credenza
long ago
in our lavender dresses

we smiled briefly
pausing with our peer
to take a recorded breath

It was all set in motion
then

The periwinkles floating still
in backyard puddles
the Spanish stucco house
the tiled roof
Long Island neighborhood
and grandma yet was
throwing the "ketz" out the kitchen window

We shared the same springy bed
next window from the skinny boy
who probably loved you so
and tho we were disallowed to cross
sister's threshold
to admire the forbidden fancy dolls
resigned to captivity
Yet we shared the tears
those crabapple summertimes at
Griffin's farm

Childhood watercolours so soon passed
like the shining rocks 'neath the clear pond
the cool fresh cowmilk on the oilcloth table
in big metal pitchers for us all to share at breakfast

Later riding atop the shoulders of our
beloved male cousins
our chicken fights were
furious fun competition

and faraway to Rockaway beach
another summer at the Indian Village
weaving from looms, we received
beaded impressions
Scrabbled phrases

Laurelton, the hunt for minnows at Twin Ponds
skinned knees and meeting friends later on
at the "Chinks"
or devouring the greasy potato knishes
at the deli that lasted a whole day in the tum

When we gangly grew it was
down to the cellars of our
best cronies
to attend our first socials
where to the end
the smiles and chances of those young lads
persist in recollection
like the lace-edged party dresses
to tell of the joy of having a beau

Remember the frozen winter's milkbox
or the sweet lick of rock candy or Charlotte Rousse?
the ponyride man
or that time to the corner drug store for candies
after raiding the penny-filled waxed cylinders
that once frothed with father's beer?

So sister, as we near the edges and
borders of things that mark our furtherness away
from all of that
prehaps those photos grow nearer and dearer in mind,
and we come back again to these shared shards

back to the Lone Ranger and the
Video Captain days
of our yesteryear
knowing where we came from is yet
who we are
and from all the patches to this
crazy quilt we huddle under
we still are finding pattern
and color and shape and
legacy…
to see what yet can be…

To the Wee Fellah

The pendulum
is a swing
for the wee fellah

Baby takes it all in
like a movie camera

His eyes record
what we cannot see
for he is learning the world
through our faces
focusing on each channel
a day at a time

A day being a month's growth
for such as he
though the calendar
stretches to
encompass his
being

Sooo Sweet

If you had given up
You would not be here today
If you had doubted

the spark from the great fire
would not have reached the branches—
the leaves of your everyday
would have only twittered to barren ground
and the fruit would not have tasted so sweet today....

To Readers

The river speaks of the wind and of the tide:

Dam the tide
and these winded poems I write you
they know not where to go
if not to you

fellow human

They seep deep
and subterranean
hiding inlets
causing fits of insomnia

They clutter and entangle
like drapes of restless vines
you cannot cut through

So harsh sometimes
you cannot touch....

Sending:

Why did you call me when
I couldn't answer?

My mind has regrets and
typographical errors and
I do not speak your java

I only sing muted lullabies
in the back of the car on
long trips when
nobody listens or remembers

Why don't you call me when
I know you are there and
I can hear you better
through all this confusion?

Your eyes are magnetized
and I have a wealth of newborn ideas
sprouting from my cornucopia

I wish I could meet you somewhere like
at a skating rink and we could
glide together and decipher codes
from the sharp lines we'd leave on the ice
and spelling wouldn't matter
when everything melted

We might see the sense to things
and that all was for good
the way it reckoned—
those lines on the ice,
the natural warmth coming on in the cold
blending the you of you and the me of me....

Changeling:

For see how we kindle our own fire
one twig at a time:
one image following another
and before you know
from nothing
a fire, like a poem
is born

See how the brain changes
its chemistry
one thought like one step
at a time—
where an interest occurs
the step lightens and
before you know it
a walk becomes and a flowering
inside the image maker manifests to
a thump and a smile and a rhythm—
and a lighter step
finds the way to
the journey's start....

Things Undone:

Washing to shore
all the small promises
that couldn't keep:
the pussycats mewling
for their milk
echoing with the sea
through your conch shell

Can take over your bed
deciding where you should go
and when
and you allow it
still

You never meant harm
but it happens
and mistakes get made
and somebody got a bruised toe
and you didn't see what went down
because so much of it hurt
and you were in your own way

But on the bench later
you have to know
where the ferris wheel landed
and where the tickets flew
and everything in such a haste

to be born
and gone
before you knew it
and you are advised to just
let it all go
even before you knew
just what it was that you had
or what had you???....

Your Wildflowers

To remember what is good
when what surfaces most strong
stings and burns—
but to remember the lush, the light—
is like the gathering of wildflowers
from the tangled woods....
you once ignored or never saw them
but you front them on the kitchen sill
in a clear blue vase
where the sun can shine through and remind you
of the color of things lovely
through all the black and white....

At Eventide

(for Steve's Latte)

There are no roses
on your pillow tonight
but for the ones
in your head and
tucked away into
your dreams
this night

The moon has come
in through your window
sought you out
and the soft sparkle
in your eye

Only the heartfelt
remains
makes all the difference
brings a moment to light

patterns on the soft carpet
playing with shadows on your wall

An opaque moon
lies down beside you
incandescence
burning a sphere
in your remembering

sees into the future
of things to come
and remains by your side
as faithful a dogship—
a light to read dreams by…

What Never Dulls

the simplest things
the things that come and go
like bubbles
not premeditated
or devised
but brief beauty
happenings
that occur
in a twinkling
and leave a little
shine
on your heart....

Printed in the United States
67035LVS00002B/55

9 781424 128655